MY COMMUNION
PRAYER

Revised Edition

Bart Tesoriero

Nihil Obstat: Right Reverend Archimandrite Francis Vivona, S.T.M.,
                     J.C.L.
Imprimatur: Most Reverend Joseph A. Pepe, D.D., J.C.D.
Date: August 4, 2011
                     The Feast of Saint John Marie Vianney

Published with the approval of the Committee on Divine Worship,
United States Conference of Catholic Bishops

Excerpts from the English translation of The Roman Missal © 2010,
International Commission on English in the Liturgy Corporation (ICEL);
the English translation of the Lenten Gospel Acclamations from Lectionary
for Mass © 1969, 1981, 1997, ICEL.
All rights reserved.

Library of Congress Control Number: 2011909037
ISBN 1-936020-03-4

TABLE OF CONTENTS

INTRODUCTION

God is a Giver! He likes to give gifts. Think about it: He has given you the gift of life. He has given you natural gifts: your health, your mental and physical abilities — even your good looks! Through Baptism, God has given you the gift of faith, His divine life in your soul. He has given you your family, your friends, your home, your possessions — we could go on and on.

One of God's greatest gifts is the gift of His Holy Spirit, because it is the gift of Himself. The Holy Spirit is God's love, the love God shares between Father and Son.

God poured out the Holy Spirit on Mary and the apostles at the first Pentecost — the birthday of the Church! Today this grace of Pentecost is passed on in the sacrament of Confirmation, to help you enjoy the fullness of God's life and witness to your faith in Jesus Christ.

We offer this book to help you prepare for and live out this gift of the Holy Spirit. It includes a brief overview of Confirmation, daily prayers, the revised Order of the Mass, the Rite of Confirmation, Preparation for Confession and Communion, a Catechesis on Confirmation, the Rosary, the Stations of the Cross, prayers to the Holy Spirit, devotional prayers, and Scripture readings — all to help you receive and grow in the Holy Spirit.

May God bless you as you begin to live as a fully initiated Catholic Christian. May He help you develop all your natural and supernatural gifts and talents to enjoy fully the life He has for you and to bring His life to others. Amen!

THE SIGN OF THE CROSS

In the name of the Father, and of the Son ✠, and of the
Holy Spirit, Amen.

THE LORD'S PRAYER

Our Father, Who art in heaven, hallowed be Thy Name;
Thy Kingdom come;
Thy Will be done on earth as it is in heaven.

Give us this day our daily bread;
and forgive us our trespasses,
as we forgive those who trespass against us;
and lead us not into temptation,
but deliver us from evil.

For the kingdom, the power,
and the glory are Yours, now and for ever. Amen.

THE HAIL MARY

Hail Mary, full of grace, the Lord is with thee.
Blessed art thou among women,
and blessed is the fruit of thy womb, Jesus.

Holy Mary, Mother of God, pray for us sinners,
now and at the hour of our death. Amen.

GLORY BE TO THE FATHER

Glory be to the Father, and to the Son, and to the Holy Spirit; as it was in the beginning, is now, and ever shall be, world without end. Amen.

AN ACT OF FAITH

O my God, I firmly believe that You are one God in three Divine Persons, Father, Son, and Holy Spirit. I believe in Jesus Christ Your Son, who became man and died for our sins, and who will come to judge the living and the dead. I believe these and all the truths which the Holy Catholic Church teaches, because You have revealed them, who can neither deceive nor be deceived. Amen.

AN ACT OF HOPE

O my God, trusting in Your infinite goodness and promises, I hope to obtain pardon of my sins, the help of Your grace, and life everlasting, through the merits of Jesus Christ, my Lord and Redeemer. Amen.

AN ACT OF LOVE

O my God, I love You above all things, with my whole heart and soul, because You are all-good and worthy of all my love. I love my neighbor as myself for love of You. I forgive all who have injured me, and I ask pardon of all whom I have injured. Amen.

MORNING OFFERING TO THE SACRED HEART

O Jesus, through the Immaculate Heart of Mary, I offer You my prayers, works, joys, and sufferings of this day, in union with the Holy Sacrifice of the Mass offered throughout the world, in reparation for all my sins, for all the intentions of Your Sacred Heart, and in particular for the intentions of our Holy Father. Amen.

MY DAILY CONSECRATION TO MARY

O Mary, My Queen and my Mother, I give myself entirely to you, and to show my devotion to you I consecrate to you this day my eyes, my ears, my mouth, my heart, my whole body without reserve. Wherefore, good Mother, as I am your own, keep me and guard me as your property and possession. Amen.

GUARDIAN ANGEL PRAYER

O Angel of God, my Guardian dear,
to whom God's love commits me here,
ever this day be at my side,
to light and guard, to rule and guide. Amen.

Watch, O Lord, with those who wake,
or watch, or weep tonight,
and give Your Angels and Saints charge
over those who sleep.
Tend Your sick ones, O Lord Christ.
Rest Your weary ones,
Bless Your dying ones,
Soothe Your suffering ones,
Pity Your afflicted ones,
Shield Your joyous ones,
And all for Your love's sake.
Amen.

—SAINT AUGUSTINE

O God, come to my assistance;
O Lord make haste to help me.

Glory be to the Father, and to the Son, and to the Holy
Spirit;
as it was in the beginning, is now and ever shall be,
world without end. Amen.

*Take a moment to review your day. Thank God for the good things
that have happened, and ask His forgiveness for any times you
have failed to love Him or others.*

Dear God, thank You for keeping me safe today and for
giving me so many blessings and graces. Please forgive all my
sins and fill me with Your love. Give me and those I love a
restful sleep. Through the intercession of Our Blessed
Mother Mary, have mercy on us that we may arise with
renewed faith, hope, and love. Amen.

CONFIRMATION IN SCRIPTURE AND SACRAMENT

THE GIFT OF THE HOLY SPIRIT

Baptism, Confirmation, and Eucharist are the Sacraments of Initiation — they establish our foundation in Christ. We are born anew, or regenerated, in Baptism, strengthened in Confirmation, and nourished with the Holy Eucharist. Through disobedience, our first parents, Adam and Eve, lost God's grace (but never His love). Through the Sacraments of Initiation, won through the obedience of Christ, God restores His grace in our souls. We are alive again!

Baptism, Confirmation, and Eucharist are not an end, but rather, a beginning: an invitation to a life of conversion, transformation, and the most exciting adventure possible: to become fully human and fully holy. Confirmation gives us the fullness of the Holy Spirit.

THE HOLY SPIRIT IN SCRIPTURE

The book of Genesis speaks of the Holy Spirit in the very first chapter of the Bible:

The earth was a formless wasteland, and darkness covered the abyss, while a mighty wind swept over the waters. –GENESIS 1:2

The "mighty wind" refers to the Holy Spirit, the love of God the Father and the Son for each other, and the love proceeding from them both. The Holy Spirit is the Third Person of this Blessed Trinity, a Person mighty, but also gentle. In the Old Testament, the Spirit spoke through the prophets, who testified that the Spirit would rest upon the Messiah and His messianic people.

Referring to the Messiah — *the anointed one* — Isaiah the prophet proclaims:

The spirit of the LORD shall rest upon him:
*   a spirit of wisdom and of understanding,*
A spirit of counsel and of strength,
*   a spirit of knowledge and of fear of the LORD,*
*   and his delight shall be the fear of the LORD.*

—ISAIAH 11:2-3

Isaiah prophesied that the Holy Spirit would rest upon Jesus, anointing Him for His ministry of teaching, healing, and redeeming the children of God. Centuries later, God sent His Holy Spirit upon Mary, who conceived Christ — *the anointed one* — in her womb. After His baptism in the Jordan and testing in the wilderness, Jesus proclaimed:

"The Spirit of the Lord is upon me,
*   because he has anointed me*
*   to bring glad tidings to the poor.*
He has sent me to proclaim liberty to captives
*   and recovery of sight to the blind,*
*   to let the oppressed go free,*
and to proclaim a year acceptable to the Lord."

—LUKE 4:18-19

At Pentecost, God sent the Holy Spirit upon Mother Mary and the disciples, filling them with the power and love of Jesus Himself. The disciples went forth boldly and confidently to proclaim the mighty works of God and to bring God's love and forgiveness to everyone. 3,000 people were baptized that very day!

THE HISTORY OF CONFIRMATION

The apostles and the early Church spread God's kingdom by passing on all the gifts Jesus had entrusted to them, including the wonderful gift of the Spirit received at Pentecost. They understood this gift as a completion, or confirmation, of Baptism, and they imparted it through the laying on of hands.

Now when the apostles in Jerusalem heard that Samaria had accepted the word of God, they sent them Peter and John, who went down and prayed for them, that they might receive the holy Spirit, for it had not yet fallen upon any of them; they had only been baptized in the name of the Lord Jesus. Then they laid hands on them and they received the holy Spirit.

—ACTS 8:14-17

This was the beginning of the sacrament of Confirmation.

By the end of the second century, Confirmation had emerged as a rite separate from Baptism. In the Latin rite, this sacrament is customarily conferred on baptized children between the age of seven and eighteen.

The ordinary minister of Confirmation is the bishop, who represents the link between the confirmed and the apostles of the Church. The bishop may delegate a priest to represent him in administering the sacrament.

Each Confirmation candidate should have a sponsor, preferably one of their Godparents, who will help them on their lifelong journey of faith.

THE RITE AND EFFECTS OF CONFIRMATION

The essential rite of Confirmation includes the anointing with oil and the laying on of hands. The bishop, or his representative, uses a special oil called sacred chrism, which is oil mixed with balsam that has been consecrated by the bishop. He lays his hand on the candidate's forehead and makes the sign of the cross, saying, "Be sealed with the Gift of the Holy Spirit." As the bishop anoints the candidate, God pours out on him or her the gift of the Holy Spirit, like that received on the first Pentecost.

Confirmation imprints an indelible spiritual mark, or character, on your soul, signifying that Jesus has sealed you with His Spirit. It roots you more deeply in divine sonship and unites you more closely to Christ. Confirmation renews and invigorates the gifts of the Holy Spirit (such as those listed in Isaiah 11:2-3 and 1 Corinthians 12:7-11) in your soul, and gives you a special power to witness to your faith publicly.

In the sacrament of Confirmation, Jesus fills you with the same Spirit that came upon Mary and the disciples at that first Pentecost. Jesus calls you first of all to Himself, that you would find in Him a true friend, who knows your hopes and dreams, your struggles and successes. Jesus wants you to feel His personal love for you, and then to share this love with others.

Jesus died, rose, and sent His Spirit so all people could receive His salvation, live a fully human and holy life, and enjoy eternal life with the Blessed Trinity in heaven. And that's Good News!

THE ORDER OF THE MASS

JESUS

Gives Himself to His Father for us
(Consecration)

Is given to us by His Father
(Communion)

"I am the bread of life;
whoever comes to me will never hunger,
whoever believes in me will never thirst."
JOHN 6:35

INTRODUCTORY RITES

ENTRANCE SONG

Together we make the Sign of the Cross:

Priest: In the name of the Father, and of the Son, and of the Holy Spirit.

People: **Amen.**

GREETING

The Priest greets us in the name of the Lord:

A Priest: The grace of our Lord Jesus Christ,
and the love of God,
and the communion of the Holy Spirit
be with you all.

Or:

B Priest: Grace to you and peace from God our Father
and the Lord Jesus Christ.

Or:

C Priest: The Lord be with you.

We reply:

People: **And with your spirit.**

THE PENITENTIAL ACT

Priest: Brethren (brothers and sisters), let us
               acknowledge our sins,
            and so prepare ourselves to celebrate the
               sacred mysteries.

A Priest and People:

            I confess to almighty God
            and to you, my brothers and sisters,
            that I have greatly sinned,
            in my thoughts and in my words,
            in what I have done and in what I have failed to do,
                        We strike our breast:
            through my fault, through my fault,
            through my most grievous fault;
                        We continue:
            therefore I ask blessed Mary ever-Virgin,
            all the Angels and Saints,
            and you, my brothers and sisters,
            to pray for me to the Lord our God.

Priest: May almighty God have mercy on us,
            forgive us our sins,
            and bring us to everlasting life.

People: **Amen.**

                        Or:

Priest: Brethren (brothers and sisters), let us
            acknowledge our sins,
            and so prepare ourselves to celebrate the
            sacred mysteries.

16

Priest: Have mercy on us, O Lord.

People: **For we have sinned against you.**

Priest: Show us, O Lord, your mercy.

People: **And grant us your salvation.**

At the end of the Act, the Priest prays:

Priest: May almighty God have mercy on us,
forgive us our sins,
and bring us to everlasting life.

People: **Amen.**

THE KYRIE

*The KYRIE, or "Lord, have mercy," is sung or said
unless it was used in the Penitential Act.*

Priest: Lord, have mercy.

People: **Lord, have mercy.**

Priest: Christ, have mercy.

People: **Christ, have mercy.**

Priest: Lord, have mercy.

People: **Lord, have mercy.**

Or:

Priest: Kyrie, eleison.

People: **Kyrie, eleison.**

Priest: Christe, eleison.

People: **Christe, eleison.**

Priest: Kyrie, eleison.

People: **Kyrie, eleison.**

THE GLORIA

G lory to God in the highest,
and on earth peace to people of good will.
We praise you,
we bless you,
we adore you,
we glorify you,
we give you thanks for your great glory,
Lord God, heavenly King,
O God, almighty Father.

Lord Jesus Christ, Only Begotten Son,
Lord God, Lamb of God, Son of the Father,
you take away the sins of the world,
    have mercy on us;
you take away the sins of the world,
    receive our prayer;
you are seated at the right hand of the Father,
    have mercy on us.

For you alone are the Holy One,
you alone are the Lord,
you alone are the Most High,
Jesus Christ,
with the Holy Spirit,
in the glory of God the Father. Amen.

THE COLLECT

Priest: Let us pray.

We pray silently with the Priest.
He then prays the Collect prayer,
preparing us for the Liturgy of the Word.

He ends the prayer:

Through our Lord Jesus Christ, your Son,
who lives and reigns with you in the unity of the
Holy Spirit,
one God, for ever and ever.

People: **Amen.**

LITURGY OF THE WORD

THE FIRST READING
God Speaks to Us through the Old Testament

At the end of the reading:

Lector: The word of the Lord.
People: **Thanks be to God.**

RESPONSORIAL PSALM
The cantor proclaims the psalm, and we respond.

THE SECOND READING
God Speaks to Us through the New Testament

At the end of the reading:

Lector: The word of the Lord.
People: **Thanks be to God.**

GOSPEL ACCLAMATION

The cantor sings the Alleluia
and we repeat it.

During Lent, instead of the Alleluia,
use one of the following or other acclamations:

Praise to you, Lord Jesus Christ, king of
endless glory!
Praise and honor to you, Lord Jesus Christ!
Glory and praise to you, Lord Jesus Christ!
Glory to you, Word of God, Lord Jesus Christ!

GOSPEL DIALOGUE

Deacon (or Priest): The Lord be with you.

People: **And with your spirit.**

Deacon (or Priest): A reading from the holy Gospel
according to N.

People: **Glory to you, O Lord.**

GOSPEL READING

The Priest or Deacon proclaims
God's Word as we listen.

At the end of the Gospel:

Deacon (or Priest): The Gospel of the Lord.

People: **Praise to you, Lord Jesus Christ.**

T   # THE HOMILY

THE PROFESSION OF FAITH

The Nicene Creed

I believe in one God,
the Father almighty,
maker of heaven and earth,
of all things visible and invisible.

I believe in one Lord Jesus Christ,
the Only Begotten Son of God,
born of the Father before all ages.
God from God, Light from Light,
true God from true God,
begotten, not made, consubstantial with the Father;
through him all things were made.
For us men and for our salvation
he came down from heaven,

(All bow during the next three lines)

and by the Holy Spirit was incarnate
    of the Virgin Mary,
and became man.

For our sake he was crucified under Pontius Pilate,
he suffered death and was buried,
and rose again on the third day
in accordance with the Scriptures.

He ascended into heaven
and is seated at the right hand of the Father.
He will come again in glory
to judge the living and the dead
and his kingdom will have no end.

I believe in the Holy Spirit, the Lord, the giver of
    life,
who proceeds from the Father and the Son,
who with the Father and the Son is adored and
    glorified,
who has spoken through the prophets.

I believe in one, holy, catholic and apostolic
    Church.
I confess one Baptism for the forgiveness of sins
and I look forward to the resurrection of the dead
and the life of the world to come. Amen.

PRAYER OF THE FAITHFUL

People: Lord, hear our prayer.

The Priest ends with a prayer:

People: **Amen.**

SIT **PRESENTATION AND PREPARATION
OF THE GIFTS**

*As the Priest thanks God, we prepare our hearts to
receive the gifts of bread and wine. They will soon
become the Body and Blood of Jesus.*

The Priest prays quietly:

Blessed are you, Lord God of all creation,
for through your goodness we have received
the bread we offer you:
fruit of the earth and work of human hands,
it will become for us the bread of life.

People: Blessed be God for ever.

*The Priest pours wine and a little water into the chalice,
praying quietly:*

By the mystery of this water and wine
may we come to share in the divinity of Christ,
who humbled himself to share in our humanity.

The Priest raises the chalice slightly, praying quietly:

Blessed are you, Lord God of all creation,
for through your goodness we have received
the wine we offer you:
fruit of the vine and work of human hands,
it will become our spiritual drink.

People: Blessed be God for ever.

INVITATION TO PRAYER

Priest: Pray, brethren (brothers and sisters),
that my sacrifice and yours
may be acceptable to God,
the almighty Father.

STAND

People: **May the Lord accept the sacrifice
at your hands
for the praise and glory of his name,
for our good,
and the good of all his holy Church.**

PRAYER OVER THE OFFERINGS

The Priest prays over the offerings. We respond:

People: **Amen.**

EUCHARISTIC PRAYER II
The Preface Dialogue

Priest: The Lord be with you.

People: **And with your spirit.**

Priest: Lift up your hearts.

People: **We lift them up to the Lord.**

Priest: Let us give thanks to the Lord our God.

People: **It is right and just.**

The Preface

We give thanks and praise to God.

It is truly right and just, our duty and our salvation,
always and everywhere to give you thanks, Father
     most holy,
through your beloved Son, Jesus Christ,
your Word through whom you made all things,
whom you sent as our Savior and Redeemer,
incarnate by the Holy Spirit and born of the Virgin.
Fulfilling your will and gaining for you a holy people,
he stretched out his hands as he endured his Passion,
so as to break the bonds of death and manifest the
     resurrection.
And so, with the Angels and all the Saints
we declare your glory,
as with one voice we acclaim:

The Sanctus

Priest and People:

Holy, Holy, Holy Lord God of hosts.
Heaven and earth are full of your glory.
Hosanna in the highest.
Blessed is he who comes in the name of the Lord.
Hosanna in the highest.

KNEEL

Invocation of the Holy Spirit

ou are indeed Holy, O Lord,
he fount of all holiness.

Make holy, therefore, these gifts, we pray,
y sending down your Spirit upon them like the
dewfall,

o that they may become for us
he Body and ✠ Blood of our Lord Jesus Christ.

The Lord's Supper

t the time he was betrayed
nd entered willingly into his Passion,
e took bread and, giving thanks, broke it,
nd gave it to his disciples, saying:

TAKE THIS, ALL OF YOU, AND EAT OF IT,
OR THIS IS MY BODY,
WHICH WILL BE GIVEN UP FOR YOU.

n a similar way, when supper was ended,
e took the chalice
nd, once more giving thanks,
e gave it to his disciples, saying:

TAKE THIS, ALL OF YOU, AND DRINK FROM IT,
OR THIS IS THE CHALICE OF MY BLOOD,
HE BLOOD OF THE NEW AND ETERNAL COVENANT,
WHICH WILL BE POURED OUT FOR YOU AND FOR MANY
OR THE FORGIVENESS OF SINS.

DO THIS IN MEMORY OF ME.

Memorial Acclamation

Priest: The mystery of faith.

People: We proclaim your Death, O Lord,
and profess your Resurrection
until you come again.

Or:

When we eat this Bread and drink this Cup,
we proclaim your Death, O Lord,
until you come again.

Or:

Save us, Savior of the world,
for by your Cross and Resurrection
you have set us free.

Therefore, as we celebrate
the memorial of his Death and Resurrection,
we offer you, Lord,
the Bread of life and the Chalice of salvation,
giving thanks that you have held us worthy
to be in your presence and minister to you.

Humbly we pray
that, partaking of the Body and Blood of Christ,
we may be gathered into one by the Holy Spirit.

Remember, Lord, your Church,
spread throughout the world,
and bring her to the fullness of charity,
together with N. our Pope and N. our Bishop
and all the clergy.

Remember also our brothers and sisters
who have fallen asleep in the hope of the
    resurrection,
and all who have died in your mercy:
welcome them into the light of your face.

Have mercy on us all, we pray,
that with the Blessed Virgin Mary, Mother of God,
with the blessed Apostles
and with all the Saints who have pleased you
     throughout the ages,
we may merit to be coheirs to eternal life,
and may praise and glorify you
through your Son, Jesus Christ.

Concluding Doxology

Priest: Through him, and with him, and in him,
          O God, almighty Father,
          in the unity of the Holy Spirit,
          all glory and honor is yours,
          for ever and ever.

People: **Amen.**

Priest: At the Savior's command
          and formed by divine teaching,
          we dare to say:

THE LORD'S PRAYER

Priest and People:

> **Our Father, who art in heaven,**
> **hallowed be thy name;**
> **thy kingdom come,**
> **thy will be done**
> **on earth as it is in heaven.**
> **Give us this day our daily bread,**
> **and forgive us our trespasses,**
> **as we forgive those who trespass against us;**
> **and lead us not into temptation,**
> **but deliver us from evil.**

Priest: Deliver us, Lord, we pray, from every evil,
          graciously grant peace in our days,
          that, by the help of your mercy,
          we may be always free from sin
          and safe from all distress,
          as we await the blessed hope
          and the coming of our Savior, Jesus Christ.

People: **For the kingdom,**
          the power and the glory are yours,
          now and for ever.

THE SIGN OF PEACE

The Priest prays for peace, ending with:

Priest: Who live and reign for ever and ever.

People: **Amen.**

Priest: The peace of the Lord be with you always.

People: **And with your spirit.**

We give one another a sign of peace.

THE FRACTION OF THE BREAD

We sing or say:

Lamb of God, you take away the sins of the world,
have mercy on us.

Lamb of God, you take away the sins of the world,
have mercy on us.

Lamb of God, you take away the sins of the world,
grant us peace.

KNEEL   THE PRAYER BEFORE COMMUNION

The Priest prays quietly:

Lord Jesus Christ, Son of the living God,
who, by the will of the Father
and the work of the Holy Spirit,
through your Death gave life to the world,
free me by this, your most holy Body and Blood,
from all my sins and from every evil;
keep me always faithful to your commandments,
and never let me be parted from you.

Or:

May the receiving of your Body and Blood,
Lord Jesus Christ,
not bring me to judgment and condemnation,
but through your loving mercy
be for me protection in mind and body
and a healing remedy.

INVITATION TO COMMUNION

Priest: Behold the Lamb of God,
behold him who takes away the sins of the world.
Blessed are those called to the supper of the Lamb.

Priest and People:

**Lord, I am not worthy
that you should enter under my roof,
but only say the word
and my soul shall be healed.**

The Priest receives the Body and Blood of Christ.

COMMUNION OF THE PEOPLE

Priest: The Body of Christ.

Communicant: **Amen.**

Priest: The Blood of Christ.

Communicant: **Amen.**

The Communion Song
We sing the Communion Song together
as we receive Communion.

Period of Silence or Song of Praise
After Communion, we thank God in silent prayer
or a song of praise.

PRAYER AFTER COMMUNION

STAND

Priest: Let us pray.
The Priest prays the Prayer after Communion, ending with:

Priest: Through Christ our Lord.

People: **Amen.**

CONCLUDING RITES

God has fed us with His Word
and the Body of Christ.
Let us go now to do good works
as we praise and bless the Lord.

THE BLESSING

Priest: The Lord be with you.

People: And with your spirit.

Priest: May almighty God bless you,
         the Father, and the Son, ✠ and the Holy Spirit.

People: Amen.

DISMISSAL

Deacon (or Priest):

A   Go forth, the Mass is ended.

B   Go and announce the Gospel of the Lord.

C   Go in peace, glorifying the Lord by your life.

D   Go in peace.

People: Thanks be to God.

The Sacrament of Confirmation is usually celebrated during Mass. The candidates typically sit together with their sponsors, reminiscent of Mary and the disciples, who gathered in the upper room after Jesus' ascension, praying together as they awaited the gift of the Holy Spirit.

THE PRESENTATION OF THE CANDIDATES

After the gospel, the pastor or another priest, deacon, or catechist, presents the candidates for Confirmation to the bishop, who then gives a brief homily, explaining the Scripture readings and giving everyone present a deeper understanding of the gift of the Holy Spirit given in Confirmation.

After the homily, the bishop asks the candidates to renew their Baptismal promises.

Bishop: Do you reject Satan and all his works and all his empty promises?

Candidates: **I do.**

Bishop: Do you believe in God, the Father almighty, creator of heaven and earth?

Candidates: **I do.**

Bishop: Do you believe in Jesus Christ, his only Son, our Lord,
who was born of the Virgin Mary,
was crucified, died, and was buried,
rose from the dead,
and is now seated at the right hand of the Father?

Candidates: **I do.**

Bishop: Do you believe in the Holy Spirit,
the Lord, the giver of life,
who came upon the apostles at Pentecost
and today is given to you sacramentally in Confirmation?

Candidates: **I do.**

Bishop: Do you believe in the holy catholic Church,
the communion of saints, the forgiveness of sins,
the resurrection of the body, and life everlasting?

Candidates: **I do.**

*The bishop gives his assent to their profession of faith and
proclaims the faith of the Church:*

This is our faith. This is the faith of the Church.
We are proud to profess it, in Christ Jesus our Lord.

All: **Amen.**

THE LAYING ON OF HANDS

The laying of hands on the candidates by the bishop and the concelebrating priests expresses the biblical gesture of calling down the gift of the Holy Spirit.

The concelebrating priests stand near the bishop, who prays facing the assembly:

My dear friends:
in baptism God our Father gave the new birth of eternal life
to his chosen sons and daughters.
Let us pray to our Father
that he will pour out the Holy Spirit
to strengthen his sons and daughters with his gifts
and anoint them to be more like Christ the Son of God.

All pray silently for a short time.

The bishop and the priests who will minister the sacrament with him lay hands upon all the candidates (by extending their hands over them). The bishop alone sings or says:

All-powerful God, Father of our Lord Jesus Christ, by water and the Holy Spirit
you freed your sons and daughters from sin
and gave them new life.
Send your Holy Spirit upon them
to be their Helper and Guide.
Give them the spirit of wisdom and understanding,
the spirit of right judgment and courage,
the spirit of knowledge and reverence.
Fill them with the spirit of wonder and awe in your presence.

We ask this through Christ our Lord.

All: **Amen.**

THE ANOINTING WITH CHRISM

Through the anointing with chrism, (aromatic oil consecrated by the bishop), the candidate receives the indelible character, the seal of the Holy Spirit, along with the grace of the Holy Spirit conforming him or her more closely to Christ.

Each candidate goes to the bishop. The one who presented the candidate places his right hand on the latter's shoulder and gives the candidate's name to the bishop; or the candidate may give his own name.

The bishop dips his right thumb in the chrism and makes the sign of the cross on the forehead of the one to be confirmed, as he says:

N., be sealed with the Gift of the Holy Spirit.

The newly confirmed responds:

Amen.

The bishop says:

Peace be with you.

The newly confirmed responds:

And also with you.

The Mass proceeds as usual.

At the end of Mass, the bishop extends his hands and sings or says:

The Lord be with you.

All: And also with you.

The deacon or minister gives the invitation in these or similar words:

Bow your heads and pray for God's blessing.

Bishop:

God our Father
made you his children by water and the Holy
Spirit:
may he bless you
and watch over you with his fatherly love.

All: **Amen.**

Bishop:

Jesus Christ the Son of God
promised that the Spirit of truth
would be with his Church forever:
may he bless you and give you courage
in professing the true faith.

All: **Amen.**

Bishop:

The Holy Spirit
came down upon the disciples
and set their hearts on fire with love:
may he bless you,
keep you one in faith and love
and bring you to the joy of God's kingdom.

All: **Amen.**

The bishop adds immediately:

May almighty God bless you,
the Father, and the Son, ✠ and the Holy Spirit.

All: **Amen.**

THE SACRAMENT OF RECONCILIATION

Jesus loves you! He created you to live with Him forever. He asks you to love God with all your heart, soul, mind, and strength, and to love others as yourself.

Sometimes we turn away from Jesus and fail to love as He asks us. This sin separates us from God. But Jesus, who died for us, loves us too much to let us remain apart. He wants very much to forgive us if only we repent. This we do through the Sacrament of Reconciliation.

EXAMINATION OF CONSCIENCE

The Ten Commandments

1. I am the Lord, Your God. You shall have no other gods before Me.

Do I pray every day? Do I worship God alone? Have I participated in any superstitious practices? Do I let the things of this world (entertainment, money, etc.) take precedence over love of God?

2. You shall not take the name of the Lord in vain.

Do I respect God's name? Do I misuse it out of frustration or anger or to impress those around me? Am I willing to stand up for God, to speak of Him with others?

3. Remember to keep holy the Lord's day.

Do I attend Mass on Sundays and Holy Days? Do I participate by praying and singing? Do I listen closely to the Scripture readings? Do I refrain from work on Sundays except when necessary, and spend time with my family?

4. Honor your Father and Mother.

God puts people in authority to care for us, protect us, and guide us. Do I obey my parents willingly? Do I help out at home? Do I respect older people?

5. You shall not kill.

Do I taunt or fight with others? Have I abused alcohol or other drugs? Do I forgive readily or do I seek revenge?

6. You shall not commit adultery.

When two people get married, they promise their mutual love to one other. God wants them to honor that promise, and He wants all of us to be pure and modest in our behavior. Do I treat my body with respect? Have I kept myself pure in thought, word, and deed?

7. You shall not steal.

Am I trustworthy and faithful to my word? Do I respect other people's property? Have I stolen or damaged what belongs to another? Have I been honest in my schoolwork?

8. You shall not lie.

Have I lied to protect myself or 'get away' with something? Have I gossiped about others or damaged their reputation in any way?

9. You shall not covet your neighbor's wife.

Marriage is a great blessing, a very special gift from God. Do I allow my parents to spend time with one another? Do I pray for my parents?

10. You shall not covet your neighbor's goods.

Am I jealous or envious of the things that others have? Am I grateful for all God has given me? Do I share with others?

PREPARATION FOR CONFESSION

PRAYER BEFORE CONFESSION

Dear Jesus, I come before You today and admit that I have
sinned against heaven and against You. I repent of my sins.
I want to walk as Your child. I want to live in freedom and
joy. I want to be fully alive, made whole by Your grace and
forgiveness. Grant me the honesty to know my sins, the
humility to confess them, and the grace to avoid them.

Dear Mother Mary, please help me make a good
Confession, and be filled with the peace of Christ. Amen.

HOW TO GO TO CONFESSION

- Make the Sign of the Cross as you say, **"Bless me Father,
  for I have sinned. It has been _____ since my last
  Confession."**
- Confess your sins.
- When you have finished, say, **"I am sorry for these and
  all my sins."**
- The priest will give you a penance, and he may offer you
  some spiritual direction.
- Pray an Act of Contrition.

AN ACT OF CONTRITION

O my God, I am heartily sorry for having offended You. I
detest all my sins because of Your just punishments, but
most of all because they offend You, my God, Who are all-
good and deserving of all my love. I firmly resolve, with the
help of Your grace, to sin no more and to avoid the near
occasions of sin. Amen.

PRAYER AFTER CONFESSION

Dear God, thank You so much for forgiving me! I feel lighter, forgiven, renewed, and ready to go on with my life. I want to walk in freedom from sin, to avoid the occasions and places that would lead me back into it. Lord, I admit I can't do it without You, so please, through the prayers of Mary, my Mother, help me to continue living in peace and joy with You and others. In Jesus' name. Amen.

COMMUNION PRAYERS

PRAYER BEFORE COMMUNION

Dear Jesus, I very much want to receive You in Holy Communion. I am sorry for the ways I have hurt You and others, O Lord, by not doing what is right. Please forgive me!

Most of all, thank You for always loving me. By the prayers of Your dear Mother Mary, make me worthy to receive You now.

May this Communion fill me with joy and peace as You come into my heart. Amen.

MY OFFERING

Dear Jesus, I offer myself to You this day as I prepare to receive You in Holy Communion. Please make me ready to receive You with all the love in my heart. Amen.

MY ACT OF PRAISE

Dear God, I worship You today, Father, Son, and Holy Spirit! Thank you for being my Father and Lover. I praise You for Who you are, Good Shepherd and King of Love. To You be praise, to You be glory, to You be thanksgiving forever and ever! Amen.

MY ACT OF LOVE

Dear Jesus, You love me so much that You have given me Your Body and Blood in Holy Communion! I love You too, Jesus. Please forgive me for the times I have not loved You or others. Help me to make a home for You in my heart, that You may be always with me. Amen.

PRAYER AFTER COMMUNION

O Jesus, You have just come to me in Holy Communion.
Your Body is living in my body.
Your Heart is beating in my heart.
You are truly present in me now.

Thank You so much for coming into my heart!
I am so glad You are here with me.
Please don't ever leave me.
I love You, Jesus.
I want to live forever with You in heaven.

Today I give myself to You.
I give You my body, my mind, my heart.
Please keep me close to Your Heart,
and bring me back to You if ever I stray from You.

Jesus, I love You. Amen.

SONG OF THANKSGIVING

Give thanks to the LORD, who is good,
  whose love endures forever.
Let the house of Israel say:
  God's love endures forever.
Let those who fear the LORD say,
  God's love endures forever.
You are my God, I give you thanks;
  my God, I offer you praise.

—Psalm 118:1-2, 4, 28

Catechesis comes from the Greek word *katekhein*: to resound. When we receive Christ, we are called to be messengers of His joy. The Holy Spirit within us causes us to resonate Christ, the Light of the world and the hope of mankind, to all! God saves us so we can save others. Pope John Paul said that only after we are transformed through the Holy Spirit should we attempt the transformation of the world.

We invite you in this section to answer each question as best you can before reading the answer. See what you know! Much of this material comes from the *Compendium of the Catechism of the Catholic Church*. We will focus on the gift of the Holy Spirit and the sacrament of Confirmation.

1. ***Why did God create me?***
God, Who is love, created me because He wanted me to share in His happiness. Though our first parents disobeyed God and fell into sin, He sent His Son to redeem and save all of us, calling us into His Church, making us His adopted children and heirs of His eternal happiness, through the work of His Holy Spirit.

2. ***How does God reveal Himself to us?***
God reveals Himself to us through His Creation, in His Word, and most completely in His Son, Jesus Christ, the Word made flesh. In the sending of His Son and the gift of His Spirit, God's revelation to us is now fully complete, although our Church must gradually grasp the full significance of this revelation over the centuries.

3. *What is God calling us to?*

God calls us to be holy — fully alive, fully human, and fully obedient to Himself. Our path to holiness goes by way of the Cross and leads to true happiness now and in eternity.

4. *How can I respond to God?*

Through the gift of grace, we respond to God with the obedience of faith. As Saint Augustine said, "I believe, in order to understand; and I understand, the better to believe."

5. *How can I know God?*

I can come to know God by spending time with Him in prayer, reading His Word, receiving His sacraments, studying the Church's teachings, and reading the lives of the saints.

6. *How can I love God?*

I can grow in love for God by believing in Jesus and receiving His love, by obeying His commandments; by turning from sin, by caring for God above everything else, and by loving others as I love myself.

7. *How can I worship God?*

I worship God by celebrating Mass and receiving Holy Communion on Sundays and, when possible, during the week, by going to Confession regularly, by praying often, and by reading His Word.

8. *Who is the Holy Spirit?*

The Holy Spirit, the Third Person of the Blessed Trinity, is the love with which the Father and the Son love each other. Jesus called the Holy Spirit the *Paraclete* — *Consoler* or *Advocate* — and the *Spirit of Truth*.

9. *What is the mission of the Holy Spirit?*

The Spirit is the Lord and Giver of Life. God sends His Spirit to give us new life as His beloved children.

10. What happened at Pentecost?

On Pentecost, Jesus poured out His Holy Spirit on Mary and the apostles. They joyfully and courageously went forth to share the Good News, inviting everyone into God's communion of love.

11. What does the Holy Spirit do in the Church?

The Spirit builds up, animates, and sanctifies the Church. As the Spirit of Love, He restores God's likeness in each of us—we 'belong' now, through the Spirit!

12. How do Christ and His Spirit act in our hearts?

Christ shares His Spirit and grace with us through the sacraments. The gifts of the Spirit produce the fruits of the Spirit within us and make us holy.

13. How do we initially receive the Holy Spirit?

We first receive the Holy Spirit in the sacrament of Baptism, which cleanses us of Original Sin, unites us with Christ, gives us sanctifying grace, and makes us members of His Body, the Church.

14. What is grace?

Grace is God's free gift of supernatural life to our souls in order that we might share in His life and love, and achieve eternal salvation — eternal union with Him in heaven. God's free gift of grace calls for our free response.

15. What are the different types of grace?

Sanctifying, or habitual, grace, makes us holy over time. It is a constantly available sharing in the life and love of God. God also gives *actual* grace for specific circumstances, *sacramental* graces proper to each sacrament, and special graces or *charisms* intended for the common good of the Church.

16. *What is a sacrament?*

The seven sacraments are outward, or perceptible, signs of grace instituted by Christ and entrusted to the Church, to give grace.

17. *What does a sacrament do for us?*

A sacrament confers the sacramental grace it signifies. Christ Himself is at work in His sacraments making us children of God, forgiving our sins, feeding us with His Body and Blood, healing us and uniting us more closely to Himself and His Church. The Holy Spirit heals us and transforms us as we receive the sacraments.

18. *What is the sacrament of Confirmation?*

The Holy Spirit came on Mary and the disciples at Pentecost, and they in turn passed on this same Spirit to the newly baptized by the laying on of hands. Confirmation is the sacramental conferral of this gift of the Holy Spirit.

19. *What is the essential rite of Confirmation?*

The essential Roman rite of Confirmation consists in the anointing with sacred chrism and the laying on of hands by the minister of Confirmation, who pronounces the words, "Be sealed with the Gift of the Holy Spirit."

20. *What is the effect of Confirmation?*

Confirmation is a special outpouring of the Holy Spirit, the grace of Pentecost, on the newly confirmed. This outpouring gives us an indelible character and produces a growth in the grace of our Baptism. Confirmation roots us more deeply as the children of God, binds us more firmly to Christ and the Church, reinvigorates the gifts of the Holy Spirit in our souls, and gives us a special strength to bear witness to our Christian faith.

21. *What are the gifts of the Holy Spirit?*

The Prophet Isaiah speaks of the Messiah, and lists the gifts of the Spirit in Isaiah 11:2-3. Thus, the gifts of the Spirit are the "permanent dispositions" of

- *Wisdom:* The gift to seek God first in all things and to see life from His perspective.
- *Understanding:* The gift of enlightenment to grasp God's truth.
- *Counsel:* The gift of guidance to make good decisions and do what pleases God.
- *Fortitude:* The gift of courage and strength to overcome all obstacles in following Jesus, including interior fear and exterior intimidation.
- *Knowledge:* The gift to know God and know myself.
- *Piety:* The gift to enjoy God and the service of God.
- *Fear of the Lord:* The gift of reverence and respect towards God.

22. *What are the fruits of the Holy Spirit?*

Just as a tree draws in nourishment to produce fruit, so the gifts of the Spirit produce in us the fruits of

- Love
- Joy
- Peace
- Patience
- Kindness
- Goodness
- Faithfulness
- Gentleness
- Self-control

(See Galatians 5:22-23.)

23. *What are the two greatest commandments?*

Jesus taught that the two greatest commandments are:

- "You shall love the Lord, your God, with all your heart, with all your soul, and with all your mind."
- "You shall love your neighbor as yourself."

—MATTHEW 22:37, 39

24. *What is prayer?*

Prayer is the raising of our mind and heart to God, in **ACTS**:
- **A**doration: Praise and worship.
- **C**ontrition: Sorrow and repentance for our sins.
- **T**hanksgiving: Giving thanks in everything.
- **S**upplication: Asking for what we need.

Prayer is our personal communication with God, our Father, His Son Jesus Christ, and their Holy Spirit who dwells in our hearts.

25. *How does Jesus teach us to pray?*

Jesus teaches us by His example and by His prayer — the *Our Father* — that God is our loving Father who only wants the best for us. Jesus teaches us to seek God daily with a pure heart, a forgiving heart, a faithful heart, and a watchful heart.

"Ask and you will receive, so that your joy may be complete." –JOHN 16:24

26. *How does the Holy Spirit help us pray?*

The Holy Spirit prays within us. Saint Paul says, "In the same way, the Spirit too comes to the aid of our weakness; for we do not know how to pray as we ought, but the Spirit itself intercedes with inexpressible groanings." —ROMANS 8:26

Therefore we should always ask the Spirit to pray with us. We recommend you memorize the prayer, *Come Holy Spirit*, found on page 58.

God does not save us in isolation. We are part of a family, the Church. In union with everyone else in the Church we fulfill our calling, our vocation. We receive from the Church the Word of God, the grace of the sacraments, and the example of holiness found in Mary and the saints.

Our faith must affect how we live. As Jesus said, "Not everyone who says to me, 'Lord, Lord,' will enter the kingdom of heaven, but only the one who does the will of my Father in heaven." —MATTHEW 7:21

Our obedience in what we do actually forms part of our worship. The Church, through the Pope and bishops, teaches us to serve God and to serve others for the good of all. The Church gives us five precepts, or rules, which specify the very minimum we need to do to love God and others.

1. You shall attend Mass on Sundays and holy days of obligation and remain free from work or activity that could impede the sanctification of such days.

2. You shall confess your sins at least once a year.

3. You shall humbly receive your Creator in Holy Communion at least during the Easter season.

4. You shall observe the days of fasting and abstinence established by the Church.

5. You shall help provide for the needs of the Church.

THE SPIRITUAL AND CORPORAL WORKS
OF MERCY

Since apostolic times, the Church has given us seven ways to care for the spiritual and physical needs of our neighbor, based on Jesus' teaching.

THE SPIRITUAL WORKS OF MERCY

1. Counsel the doubtful
2. Instruct the ignorant
3. Admonish sinners
4. Comfort the afflicted
5. Forgive offenses
6. Bear wrongs patiently
7. Pray for the living and the dead

THE CORPORAL WORKS OF MERCY

1. Feed the hungry
2. Give drink to the thirsty
3. Clothe the naked
4. Shelter the homeless
5. Visit the sick
6. Visit those in prison
7. Bury the dead

COME HOLY SPIRIT

Come, Holy Spirit, fill the hearts of Your faithful,
and kindle in us the fire of Your Love.
Send forth Your Spirit and we shall be created,
and You shall renew the face of the earth.

Let us pray. O God, who by the light of Your Holy Spirit,
has instructed the hearts of Your faithful, grant us by the
same Spirit to be truly wise and ever to rejoice in Your
consolation, through the same Christ our Lord, Amen.

PRAYER FOR THE GIFTS OF THE SPIRIT

Lord and Giver of Life, Father of the Poor,
You who pour forth Your Sevenfold gifts
through the Sacrament of Confirmation, hear us as we pray:
Spirit of sonship, grant to us **Fear of the Lord** that we
might stand in Your presence with wonder and awe,
and **Piety** to draw our hearts to recognize
that You are our Father and we are Your children.

Keep us in step with You by sending us
Counsel to know Your will for our lives; **Wisdom** to apply
that will; and **Fortitude** to do Your will.

Spirit that leads us to all truth,
grant us **Knowledge** to know Your truth in our heart,
and **Understanding** to comprehend what You have
revealed.

Heavenly Father, may these gifts conform us to the image of
your Son, Jesus, the firstborn among many.

In Jesus' name. Amen.

PRAYER FOR THE FRUITS OF THE SPIRIT

Holy Spirit, eternal Love of the Father and the Son,
I come into Your presence. Please come upon me,
O Spirit of Jesus, and produce in me the fruit of love,
that I may be united to You by divine love;
joy, that I may be filled with Your consolation;
peace, that I may enjoy tranquility of soul;
and patience, that I may endure everything
that may be opposed to my own desires.

Divine Spirit, infuse in me the fruit of kindness,
that I may willingly help others;
goodness, that I may be compassionate toward all;
long-suffering, that I may not be discouraged
but may persevere in prayer; and gentleness,
that I may be even-tempered with others.

Spirit of God, graciously impart to me the fruit of
faithfulness,
that I may have confidence in the Word of God, and true
modesty and chastity, that I may keep my body pure.

O Holy Spirit, help me keep my heart pure, that I may
enjoy Your friendship both now and in the glory of Your
kingdom with the Father and the Son. Amen.

BREATHE IN ME, O HOLY SPIRIT

Breathe in me, O Holy Spirit, that my thoughts may all be holy.
Act in me, O Holy Spirit, that my work, too, may be holy.
Draw my heart, O Holy Spirit, that I love but what is holy.
Strengthen me, O Holy Spirit, to defend all that is holy.
Guard me, then, O Holy Spirit, that I always may be holy.
Amen. —St. Augustine

DAILY CONSECRATION TO THE HOLY SPIRIT

O Holy Spirit, divine Spirit of light and love, I consecrate to You my understanding, my heart and my will, my whole being, for time and eternity. May I always follow Your heavenly inspirations and the teachings of the Catholic Church, which You guide in all truth. May my heart be ever inflamed with love of God and others. May I conform my will to Your Will, and may my whole life be a faithful imitation of the life and virtues of our Lord and Savior, Jesus Christ, to Whom, with the Father and You, be honor and glory forever. Amen.

PRAYER FOR THE INDWELLING OF THE SPIRIT

Holy Spirit, powerful Consoler, sacred Bond of the Father and the Son, Hope of the afflicted, come into my heart and establish Your Kingdom in me. Enkindle in me the fire of Your Love so that I may be wholly surrendered to You.

When You dwell in us, You also prepare a dwelling for the Father and the Son. Please come to me, Consoler of abandoned souls, and Protector of the needy. Help the afflicted, strengthen the weak, and support the wavering.

Come and purify me. Let no evil desire take possession of me. You love the humble and resist the proud. Come to me, glory of the living, and hope of the dying. Lead me by Your grace that I may always be pleasing to You. Amen.

PRAYER FOR THE OUTPOURING OF THE HOLY SPIRIT

Dear Spirit of Jesus, we ask for an outpouring of Your graces, blessings and gifts, upon those who do not believe, that they may believe;

Upon those who are doubtful or confused, that they may understand;

Upon those who are lukewarm or indifferent, that they may be transformed;

Upon those who are living in the state of sin, that they may be converted;

Upon those who are weak, that they may be strengthened;
Upon those who are holy, that they may persevere. Amen.

PRAYER TO RENEW THE GRACE OF MY CONFIRMATION

Dear Holy Spirit, thank You for coming into my heart in a special way on my Confirmation Day, when I was signed with sacred chrism and sealed with Your gift of grace. I praise, worship, and enjoy You! You make my soul Your home, You help me fight against evil, and You give me the victory won through Jesus' Passion, Death, and Resurrection.

O Holy Spirit, renew in me the grace of my Confirmation. Let me feel again Your love, peace, and joy. Forgive me for any ways I have grieved You or sinned against You, and give me the grace of a repentant and humble heart.

Inflame me again with Your fire of love, O Holy Spirit, that I may be a light in this world. Help me witness by my life to Jesus' love, and in so doing, to lead others to Him.

I ask all this, dear Spirit of God, through the intercession of Mary, the Mother of Jesus and Your Spouse, for Your glory and the good of all humanity. Amen.

When we pray, we speak to God, vocally or silently, and listen to Him in our hearts. He wants us to get to know and love Him. In the Rosary we pray to God with Mary, the Mother of Jesus, and our Mother as well. As we pray the prayers of the Rosary, we reflect on significant events, or mysteries, in the lives of Jesus and Mary. The complete Rosary consists of four groups of five mysteries each. These are the Joyful, Luminous, Sorrowful and Glorious Mysteries.

As we pray the Rosary, we try to imagine what was happening in each mystery and what God wants to teach us. We want to grow closer to Him and learn how He wants us to live. But even more, to pray the Rosary is to hold Mary's hand and let her bring us to Jesus. When we are with Jesus and Mary, we know the peace, love, and joy of God.

HOW TO PRAY THE ROSARY

- Begin by making the Sign of the Cross ✠ and praying *The Apostles' Creed* while you hold the crucifix.

- Pray one *Our Father* on the first bead, three *Hail Marys* on the next three beads for the virtues of Faith, Hope, and Charity, and finish with a *Glory Be.*

- Announce the first Mystery and think about it while praying an *Our Father* on the large bead, ten *Hail Marys* on the smaller beads, and finishing with a *Glory Be*. This is one decade.

- If you wish, you may add the *Fatima Prayer* after the *Glory Be*:

"O My Jesus, forgive us our sins, save us from the fires of hell. Lead all souls to heaven, especially those most in need of Your mercy."

Continue in this way until all you have prayed all five decades. To finish, pray the *Hail Holy Queen*.

HAIL, HOLY QUEEN

Hail, Holy Queen, Mother of Mercy, our life, our sweetness, and our hope!
To thee do we cry, poor banished children of Eve; to thee do we send up our sighs, mourning and weeping in this valley of tears!

Turn then, most gracious Advocate, thine eyes of mercy toward us; and after this, our exile, show unto us the blessed fruit of thy womb, Jesus.

O clement,
O loving,
O sweet Virgin Mary.

V. Pray for us, O holy Mother of God.

R. That we may be made worthy of the promises of Christ.

THE JOYFUL MYSTERIES

THE ANNUNCIATION

Then the angel said to her, "Do not be afraid, Mary, for you have found favor with God. Behold, you will conceive in your womb and bear a son, and you shall name him Jesus."
—LUKE 1:30-31

The Angel Gabriel told Mary that God had chosen her from all women to be the Mother of His Son. Mary said 'Yes' to God. Because of this, God could become man, and all people could be saved.

Mary believed and trusted God even when it was hard to understand. She obeyed God knowing He always works everything out for the good.

Dear Mother Mary, help us also say yes to God with a willing heart.

THE VISITATION

When Elizabeth heard Mary's greeting, the infant leaped in her womb, and Elizabeth, filled with the holy Spirit, cried out in a loud voice and said, "Most blessed are you among women, and blessed is the fruit of your womb." —LUKE 1:41-42

When Mary heard that her cousin Elizabeth was pregnant, she went quickly to visit and help her. Elizabeth was overjoyed to see Mary.

One of the best ways to make others happy is to visit them. In this way, we help bring the love of Jesus to others, just as Mary brought the love of Jesus to Elizabeth and her unborn child.

Dear Mother Mary, thank you for teaching us to be good to others. Help us always bring them joy, that they will feel the love of Jesus.

THE BIRTH OF JESUS

While they were there, the time came for her to have her child, and she gave birth to her firstborn son. She wrapped him in swaddling clothes and laid him in a manger, because there was no room for them in the inn. —LUKE 2:6-7

Long ago in Bethlehem, Mary gave birth to Jesus and laid him in a manger. The angels sang, "Glory to God in the highest, and peace to His people on earth!"

Dear Mother Mary, help us to feel Jesus' love for us, and to love one another as well.

THE PRESENTATION OF JESUS

*"Now, Master, you may let your servant go
    in peace, according to your word,
for my eyes have seen your salvation,
    which you prepared in sight of all the peoples,
a light for revelation to the Gentiles,
    and glory for your people Israel."* —LUKE 2:29-32

God promised Simeon that he would not die until he had seen the Messiah.

God always keeps His promises, even when we have to wait a long time.

Dear Mother Mary, help us, like Simeon, trust that God will keep all His promises and bring us His salvation.

THE FINDING OF JESUS

"Why were you looking for me? Did you not know that I must be in my Father's house?" But they did not understand what he said to them. —LUKE 2:49-50

Jesus always did his Father's Will, even when others did not understand. Even so, he returned home with his parents and obeyed them.

Dear Mother Mary, help us to obey our parents, as Jesus did, and to love God with all our hearts.

Thursday

THE BAPTISM OF JESUS IN THE JORDAN

After all the people had been baptized and Jesus also had been baptized and was praying, heaven was opened and the holy Spirit descended upon him in bodily form like a dove. And a voice came from heaven, "You are my beloved Son; with you I am well pleased." —LUKE 3:21-22

Jesus obeyed his Father always, because he loved Him. Jesus teaches us to always begin our day with prayer, that we also may obey our Heavenly Father.

Dear Mother Mary, it is good to know my Heavenly Father loves me as He loves Jesus. Please pray that I will obey Him as Jesus did.

THE WEDDING AT CANA

And when the headwaiter tasted the water that had become wine ... the headwaiter called the bridegroom and said to him, "Everyone serves good wine first, and then when people have drunk freely, an inferior one; but you have kept the good wine until now." —JOHN 2:9-10

Jesus changed water into wine to serve others. In so doing, he revealed his glory. Mary teaches us in this mystery to do whatever her Son tells us.

Dear Mother Mary, when you asked Him, Jesus changed water into wine and opened the hearts of His followers to faith. Help me also trust in God in all that I do.

JESUS PROCLAIMS GOD'S KINGDOM

After John had been arrested, Jesus came to Galilee proclaiming the gospel of God: "This is the time of fulfillment. The kingdom of God is at hand. Repent, and believe in the gospel."
—MARK 1:14-15

Jesus proclaimed the good news that God was calling all people to come back to Him. We can only change our hearts with God's help.

Dear Mother Mary, help me to hear Jesus in His Word and in the quiet of my heart. Help me to obey Him and to love with His love.

THE TRANSFIGURATION OF JESUS

[Jesus] took Peter, John, and James and went up the mountain to pray. While he was praying, his face changed in appearance and his clothing became dazzling white. ... Then from the cloud came a voice that said, "This is my chosen Son; listen to him."
—LUKE 9:28-29, 35

Jesus calls us to be the light of the world. When we obey Jesus, His light shines through us. In this way we bring light to everyone!

Dear Mother Mary, you always let the Lord shine His light in you and in your life. Help me listen to Jesus and let His light shine in my heart.

THE INSTITUTION OF THE EUCHARIST

When the hour came, he ... took the bread, said the blessing, broke it, and gave it to them, saying, "This is my body, which will be given for you; do this in memory of me." And he did the same with the cup after they had eaten, saying, "This cup is the new covenant in my blood, which will be shed for you." —LUKE 22:14, 19-20

Jesus loved us so much that he gave himself so he could always be with us. May Mary help us always prepare a place for Jesus in our hearts.

Dear Mother Mary, thank you for sharing your Son with us so He could bring us His life. May we always be thankful for the gift of His Body and Blood.

Tuesday, Friday

THE AGONY IN THE GARDEN

Then they came to a place called Gethsemane... . ... and [Jesus] began to be troubled and distressed. —MARK 14:32-33

In the Garden of Gethsemane the night before he died, Jesus' friends fell asleep and he was all alone. He felt afraid, lonely, and very sad. Jesus prayed hard for his Father's help.

Jesus placed all his trust and confidence in his Heavenly Father, as he had his whole life. Even when bad things happen, God will always take care of us.

Dear Mother Mary, please help me to remember Jesus and spend time with Him in prayer.

JESUS IS SCOURGED AT THE PILLAR

So Pilate, wishing to satisfy the crowd, released Barabbas to them and, after he had Jesus scourged, handed him over to be crucified. —MARK 15:15

The soldiers arrested Jesus and put him in prison. Pontius Pilate, who was afraid of the people, ordered the soldiers to whip Jesus even though he had done nothing wrong.

The soldiers hurt Jesus very much. Yet during all this time, Jesus was thinking of us. He offered his suffering so we could someday come to heaven to be with him forever.

Dear Mother Mary, please help me to love others even when they are not kind to me. May Jesus live in my heart today.

JESUS IS CROWNED WITH THORNS

The soldiers wove a crown out of thorns and placed it on his head, and clothed him in a purple robe, and they came to him and said, "Hail, King of the Jews!" —JOHN 19:2-3

The soldiers hurt Jesus very much, but he suffered all this in silence. Jesus knew that someday his kingdom would come. He did not strike back at those who hurt him, but offered his suffering up for them and for all people.

Dear Mother Mary, help me let Jesus love others through me.

JESUS CARRIES THE CROSS

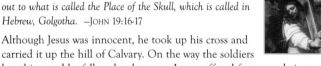

So they took Jesus, and carrying the cross by himself, he went out to what is called the Place of the Skull, which is called in Hebrew, Golgotha. —JOHN 19:16-17

Although Jesus was innocent, he took up his cross and carried it up the hill of Calvary. On the way the soldiers beat him, and he fell under the cross. Jesus suffered for us, and gives us the strength to follow him.

Dear Mary, you were very sad when you saw your son carrying the cross. When He saw you He felt stronger. Help me assist others who may be hurting.

JESUS DIES ON THE CROSS

After they had crucified him, they divided his garments by casting lots; then they sat down and kept watch over him there. —MATTHEW 27:35-36

As he hung on the cross, Jesus forgave his enemies. He gave us Mary to be our Mother, and gave us to Mary as her children. When everything was finished, Jesus bowed his head and died.

Dear Mother Mary, you were heartbroken when Jesus died, but you knew He did it for us. Thank you for sharing your Son with us all.

THE GLORIOUS MYSTERIES

Sunday, Wednesday

THE RESURRECTION OF JESUS

Then the angel said to the women in reply, "Do not be afraid! I know that you are seeking Jesus the crucified. He is not here, for he has been raised just as he said. Come and see the place where he lay." —MATTHEW 28:5-6

After three days, Jesus arose from the dead! He won! He did it for us, so we could share in His victory over sin and death. Alleluia!

Dear Mother Mary, thank you for giving us your Son Jesus, who rose from the dead so we could always be with Him.

THE ASCENSION OF JESUS

As he blessed them, he parted from them and was taken up to heaven. —LUKE 24:51

Forty days after His Resurrection, Jesus gathered His disciples together. He told them to wait in Jerusalem until they received power from heaven. After Jesus blessed them, He was taken up into heaven.

Dear Mother Mary, help us to stay close to Jesus and bring His love to everyone.

THE DESCENT OF THE HOLY SPIRIT

When the time for Pentecost was fulfilled ... suddenly there came from the sky a noise like a strong driving wind, and it filled the entire house in which they were. ... And they were all filled with the holy Spirit. —ACTS 2:1-4

On Pentecost, the Holy Spirit filled the disciples with faith and courage to bring God's love and forgiveness to all people.

Dear Mother Mary, you are filled with the Holy Spirit. Please pray that the Spirit will fill me with His fire of love. Amen.

THE ASSUMPTION OF MARY

Mary said: "My soul proclaims the greatness of the Lord; / and my spirit rejoices in God my savior. / ...The Mighty One has done great things for me, / and holy is his name." —LUKE 1:46-47, 49

Mary always said 'Yes' to God. God gave Mary a special gift at the end of her life. Jesus took His Mother, body and soul, to be in heaven with Him, forever.

Dear Mother Mary, please help me to love God that I may live forever with Him. Amen.

THE CROWNING OF MARY

"He has helped his servant Israel, / remembering his mercy." —LUKE 1:54-55

Adam and Eve disobeyed God, and lost His grace. Mary obeyed God, and through Jesus we have received God's grace back into our souls. Mary is our Heavenly Mother. She is very powerful and is always able to help us when we call on her.

Dear Mother Mary, please wrap us in your arms of love that we may always be close to God and bring others to rejoice in His salvation. In Jesus' Name. Amen!

On Good Friday, Jesus suffered and died to take away our sins. The Stations of the Cross help us remember the journey Jesus took to Calvary for our sake. At the beginning of each station, pray:

V. We adore You, O Christ, and we praise You.

R. Because by Your holy Cross, You have redeemed the world.

1. JESUS IS CONDEMNED TO DEATH

It was preparation day for Passover, and it was about noon. And he said to the Jews, "Behold, your king!" They cried out, "Take him away, take him away! Crucify him!" Pilate said to them, "Shall I crucify your king?" The chief priests answered, "We have no king but Caesar." Then he handed him over to them to be crucified. —JOHN 19:14-16

After the Last Supper, Jesus went out with his disciples to the Garden of Gethsemane to pray. There he was betrayed by Judas, who brought soldiers to arrest Jesus. He was taken to prison, and the next day Pontius Pilate, the Roman Governor, had Jesus scourged and crowned with thorns. He knew Jesus was innocent but he was afraid of the crowds. So he condemned Jesus to die on the cross.

**Jesus, when I am afraid,
please help me to trust in You.**

2. JESUS ACCEPTS HIS CROSS

Then he handed him over to them to be crucified. So they took Jesus, and carrying the cross himself he went out to what is called the Place of the Skull, in Hebrew, Golgotha.
—JOHN 19:16-17

Jesus saw the soldiers bringing the heavy cross for him to carry. He was innocent, yet he chose to carry this cross for all of us, to set us free.

Jesus, teach me to obey God even when it is very hard, even when I am treated unfairly.

3. JESUS FALLS THE FIRST TIME

We had all gone astray like sheep,
each following his own way;
But the LORD laid upon him
the guilt of us all. —ISAIAH 53:6

The cross was very heavy and Jesus was very weak after his beating. He fell under the cross and the soldiers beat him until he stood up once again.

Jesus, teach me to keep going even when I feel like giving up. You are always with me.

4. JESUS MEETS HIS MOTHER MARY

Come, all you who pass by the way;
*   look and see*
Whether there is any suffering like my
*   suffering.*
—LAMENTATIONS 1:12

As Jesus struggled under the heavy cross, he looked into the crowd of angry people. Suddenly he saw his mother! How she wanted to hold him and kiss him and comfort him! How he wanted to hold her and comfort her! They looked at each other with great love, and then the soldiers pushed him on his way.

Jesus, help me stay close to Mary,
for then I will be close to You.

5. SIMON HELPS JESUS CARRY THE CROSS

As they led him away they took hold of a certain Simon, a Cyrenian, who was coming in from the country; and after laying the cross on him, they made him carry it behind Jesus.
—LUKE 23:26

The soldiers were afraid that Jesus would die before they reached Calvary. So they pulled a man out of the crowd, laid the cross on him, and made him carry it behind Jesus.

Help me, Jesus, to help those who need me.

6. VERONICA WIPES THE FACE OF JESUS

He was spurned and avoided by men,
a man of suffering, accustomed to infirmity.
—ISAIAH 53:3

All his life, Jesus had helped other people. Now, in his time of trouble, a woman named Veronica reached out to wipe his face. She felt afraid of the soldiers but she helped Jesus anyway. She dried away the sweat and blood, and Jesus was very thankful.

Jesus, help me to be not afraid to do good.

7. JESUS FALLS THE SECOND TIME

I was hard pressed and falling,
but the LORD came to my help.
—PSALM 118:13

Jesus was growing weaker and weaker. He wanted to keep going but his legs gave way beneath him and he fell a second time. The crowd laughed at him and shoved him as he struggled to get up and keep going. Still he loved them all.

Jesus, help me to follow You
even when others laugh at me.

8. JESUS MEETS THE WOMEN OF JERUSALEM

"Daughters of Jerusalem, do not weep for me; weep instead for yourselves and for your children." —LUKE 23:28

Some women from Jerusalem came out, crying, to meet Jesus. Jesus told them to weep instead for themselves and their children, because if the Son of God had to suffer so much, what would happen to those who turned away from him?

Jesus, help me stay close to You.

9. JESUS FALLS THE THIRD TIME

He humbled himself,
becoming obedient to death,
even death on a cross.
—PHILIPPIANS 2:8

As Jesus climbed the hill of Calvary, he fell one last time. He could hardly lift his head. Yet he knew he had to die for us on the cross, so with one final effort he got up and finished his journey.

Jesus, Your love for us kept You going.
Help me to believe in Your love for me
and to always get up when I make mistakes.

10. JESUS IS STRIPPED OF HIS GARMENTS

They divide my garments among them;
for my clothing they cast lots. —PSALM 22:19

Finally Jesus came to the top of Mount Calvary. The soldiers stripped his clothes off him, and prepared to nail him to the cross. Jesus allowed them to do this to him because he loved you and me.

Jesus, help me be strong when others are weak.

11. JESUS IS NAILED TO THE CROSS

When they came to the place called the Skull,
they crucified him and the criminals there,
one on his right, the other on his left.
—LUKE 23:33

The soldiers nailed Jesus' hands and feet to the cross. Then they raised the cross up so everyone could see him. Jesus hung there in front of the crowd, loving them even as they crucified him.

Jesus, help me be silent when I feel like complaining.

12. JESUS DIES UPON THE CROSS

Jesus cried out in a loud voice, "Father, into your hands I commend my spirit"; and when he had said this he breathed his last.
—LUKE 23:46

Jesus hung on the cross for three hours. He offered his suffering for all of us, that we might be able to enter heaven and enjoy eternal life with God. He died so we could have the power to love one another as he loved us. In the end, Jesus won the battle over sin and death.

Jesus, thank You for dying for us.
Thank You for giving us the grace to be free from sin.
Help us to follow You always.

13. JESUS IS TAKEN DOWN FROM THE CROSS

They shall look on him whom they have thrust through, and they shall mourn for him as one mourns for an only son. —ZECHARIAH 12:10

Jesus' friends gently took him off the cross, and placed his body in the arms of Mary. Mary used to rock Jesus gently in her arms and sing to him when he was a little baby. Now as she cradled him again, only God knew the sorrow in her heart.

Mary, sometimes I am very sad, too.
Help me remember you are always near,
and you will hold me as you held your only Son.

4. JESUS IS PLACED IN THE TOMB

They took the body of Jesus and bound it with burial cloths along with the spices ... .
. They laid Jesus there because of the Jewish reparation day; for the tomb was close by.
JOHN 19:40, 42

Jesus was born in a stable that belonged to someone else and buried in a tomb not his own. His mother Mary and his friends washed his body and covered it with spices and clean cloths. Then they rolled a great stone over the entrance to the tomb.

Jesus, I trust in You.

5. JESUS RISES FROM THE DEAD!

He said to them, "Do not be amazed! You seek Jesus of Nazareth, the crucified. He has been raised; he is not here. Behold, the place where they laid him." —MARK 16:6

The tomb could not hold Jesus! On the third day, just as He said, Jesus rose from the dead. A new light of joy and peace dawned in Mary's heart and in the hearts of His disciples.

Jesus, I receive Your Resurrection Life in my heart today!

In 1931, a Polish nun, Sister Faustina Kowalska, saw a vision of Jesus, clothed in white with His arm raised in blessing. Two rays, symbolizing His Blood, the life of our souls, and the water which cleanses our souls, streamed out of His heart. Jesus told Sister Faustina to paint an image portraying His Divine Mercy and to spread the Image and Message of Mercy throughout the world: *God loves each of us and His Mercy is greater than all our sins!*

Jesus taught Sister Faustina the ABCs of Mercy:

Ask for God's mercy — daily.

Be merciful to others — constantly.

Completely trust in God's mercy — always.

Although Sister Faustina died at the early age of 33, she lived in such a way that everyone who encountered her went away happy and joyful. Pope John Paul II canonized Saint Faustina as the first saint of the new millennium, in April 2000, at Saint Peter's Basilica.

The more we trust Jesus, the more mercy we will receive. Through Jesus' passion and death, God has made available for all people an ocean of mercy.

Some ways you can show mercy to others are through the Spiritual and Corporal works of mercy. (See page 57)

Jesus told Saint Faustina that His heart was the fountain of mercy, the water flowing out was His mercy, and the container for the water is our trust. The water is there for us, and no one is excluded. All we need do is pray, trust, and act.

THE CHAPLET OF DIVINE MERCY

For private recitation on ordinary rosary beads

Our Father...,
Hail Mary...,
the Apostles' Creed.

Then, on the Our Father beads you will say the following words:

Eternal Father, I offer You the Body and Blood, Soul and Divinity of Your dearly beloved Son, Our Lord Jesus Christ, in atonement for our sins and those of the whole world.

On the Hail Mary beads you will say the following words:

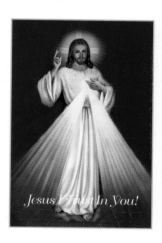

Jesus I Trust In You!

For the sake of His sorrowful Passion, have mercy on us and on the whole world.

In conclusion three times you will recite these words:

Holy God, Holy Mighty One, Holy Immortal One, have mercy on us and on the whole world.

Jesus appeared to Sister Margaret Mary Alacoque in France in 1675, showing her His Sacred Heart, on fire with love for us and desiring our love in return. Jesus promised Saint Margaret Mary that He would help those who honor His Sacred Heart. He also said, "I will bless every home in which an image of My Heart will be honored."

Jesus asks us to love Him fervently, pray to Him constantly, trust Him in everything, visit him in the Blessed Sacrament frequently, and receive Him in the Holy Eucharist as much as possible.

CONSECRATION TO THE SACRED HEART OF JESUS

Dear Jesus, my Redeemer, look down upon me today. I want to serve You, and therefore I freely consecrate myself today to Your most Sacred Heart. Have mercy on us all, most merciful Jesus, and draw us all to Your Sacred Heart.

Grant, O Lord, to Your Church freedom and protection; give Your peace and mercy to all nations, and make the earth resound with one cry: "Praised be Jesus Christ, who has won our salvation! To Him be glory and honor forever." Amen.

Look down upon me, good and gentle Jesus, while before Your face I humbly kneel and, with burning soul, pray and beseech You to fix deep in my heart lively sentiments of faith, hope, and charity;

true contrition for my sins,

and a firm purpose of amendment;

While I contemplate, with great love and tender pity,

Your five most precious wounds,

pondering over them within me
and calling to mind the words which David, Your prophet, said of You, my Jesus:

"They have pierced my hands and my feet,
They numbered all my bones."

Amen.

MARY, WOMAN OF FAITH

Mary was most likely a teen when the archangel Gabriel appeared to her with astonishing news: "God has chosen you to be the mother of His Son." You can imagine her shock and amazement! Mary asked the angel how this could happen. Gabriel replied that the Holy Spirit would come upon her, and overshadow her. Mary replied, "May it be done to me according to your word." —LUKE 1:38

Mary's 'Yes' didn't stop there. She obeyed God faithfully all her life. At the Cross, even though Mary loved Jesus more than any one else ever could, she offered him up to the Father — out of love for us. From the Cross, Jesus gave her to us, to be our spiritual mother. Mary was with the apostles in the upper room — the cenacle — on Pentecost, when God sent the Holy Spirit upon her and the disciples, filling them with the power and love of Jesus Himself.

PRAYER TO OUR LADY OF THE CENACLE

Mary Immaculate, our Mother, most holy Virgin of the Cenacle, obtain for me the gifts of the Holy Spirit, that under your guidance and teaching, I may live in love and persevere in prayer for the greater glory of God. May I labor by both word and deed for the salvation of souls, and deserve to enter into everlasting life. Graciously be near me in my present needs, our Lady of the Cenacle, and help me by your power, so that almighty God may be pleased to grant me, through your prayers, the favor for which I now earnestly pray (mention your intention).

Mary, Queen of the Apostles, pray for us.

THE ANGELUS

The Angelus began as a morning greeting to Mary. It is now prayed at 8 AM, Noon, and 6 PM.

V. The Angel of the Lord declared unto Mary.

R. And she conceived by the Holy Spirit. (*Hail Mary*)

V. Behold the handmaid of the Lord.

R. Be it done unto me according to thy word. (*Hail Mary*)

V. And the Word was made Flesh.

R. And dwelt among us. (*Hail Mary*)

V. Pray for us, O Holy Mother of God.

R. That we may be made worthy of the promises of Christ.

Let us pray: Pour forth, we beseech Thee, O Lord, Thy grace into our hearts; that we to whom the Incarnation of Christ, Thy Son, was made known by the message of an Angel, may by His Passion and Cross, be brought to the glory of His Resurrection. Through the same Christ our Lord. Amen.

THE MEMORARE

Remember, O most gracious Virgin Mary, that never was it known, that any one who fled to thy protection, implored thy help, or sought thy intercession, was left unaided. Inspired by this confidence, I fly unto thee, O Virgin of virgins my Mother; to thee do I come, before thee I stand, sinful and sorrowful. O Mother of the Word Incarnate, despise not my petitions, but in thy mercy hear and answer me. Amen.

THE BROWN SCAPULAR DEVOTION

What is the Brown Scapular?

The Brown Scapular consists of two small pieces of cloth, typically wool, connected by two long cords worn over the head and resting on the shoulders.

What is the history of the Brown Scapular?

According to tradition, over 700 years ago Our Blessed Mother appeared to Saint Simon Stock, holding out to him a brown woolen scapular. *"Receive My beloved son, the Scapular of thy Order. ...Whoever dies invested with this Scapular shall be preserved from the eternal flames. It is a sign of salvation, a sure safeguard in danger, a pledge of peace and of My special protection until the end of the ages."* The Scapular, then, is a special garment worn as a sign of love and devotion to Mary our Mother and Queen.

What are the conditions of wearing a brown Scapular?

- Wear the Brown Scapular continuously
- Observe chastity according to one's state in life.
- Pray daily the "Little Office of the Blessed Virgin Mary."
- You may substitute any of the following:
  - To observe the fasts of the Church.
  - To pray five decades of the Holy Rosary
  - or with the permission of a priest to do a good work.

To wear the Brown Scapular is to trust in Our Lady who has great power of intercession before her Son. It is always a powerful means of grace because it always assures us of Mary's continuous prayers.

NOVENA PRAYER TO SAINT JOSEPH

This prayer is over 1900 years old. Pray it for nine consecutive mornings for anything you may desire. It has never been known to fail.

O Saint Joseph, whose protection is so great, so strong, so prompt before the Throne of God, I place in you all my interests and desires.

O Saint Joseph, please help me by your powerful intercession and obtain for me from your Divine Son all spiritual blessings through Jesus Christ, Our Lord; so that having engaged here below your Heavenly power I may offer my thanksgiving and praise to the most loving of Fathers.

O Saint Joseph, I never weary contemplating you and Jesus asleep in your arms. I dare not approach while He reposes near your heart. Press Him in my name and kiss His fine Head for me, and ask Him to return the Kiss when I draw my dying breath. Saint Joseph, Patron of departing souls, pray for us. Amen.

This prayer was found in the fiftieth year of Our Lord Jesus Christ. In the 1500's it was sent by the Pope to Emperor Charles when he was going into battle.

Whoever reads this prayer, hears it or carries it, will never die a sudden death, nor be drowned, nor will poison take effect on them. They will not fall into the hands of the enemy nor be burned in any fire, nor will they be defeated in battle.

PRAYER TO SAINT MICHAEL

Saint Michael the Archangel, defend us in battle. Be our safeguard against the wickedness and snares of the devil. May God rebuke him, we humbly pray; and do you, O Prince of the heavenly host, by the power of God cast into hell Satan and all the evil spirits who wander through the world seeking the ruin of souls. Amen.

SPIRITUAL ARMOR PRAYER
Based on Ephesians 6:13-17

Heavenly Father, we ask You today for Your truth as a belt tight around our loins. We put on the zeal to announce Your good news of peace as shoes for our feet. We put on Your righteousness, O Christ, as our breastplate, and the hope of salvation as a helmet for our head. Father, we take up faith as a shield which is able to put out all the fiery darts of the enemy, and the sword of the Spirit, which is Your Word, O Lord. Father, may the love with which You have loved Jesus be in us, and may Jesus be in us. We ask You for the grace of a servant heart. Amen.

PRAYER OF SAINT FRANCIS

Lord, make me
an instrument of Your peace.
Where there is hatred,
let me sow love;
where there is injury, pardon;
where there is doubt, faith;
where there is despair, hope;
where there is darkness, light;
and where there is sadness, joy.

O Divine Master, grant
that I may not so much seek
to be consoled as to console;
to be understood as to
understand;
to be loved as to love;
for it is in giving that we
receive;
it is in pardoning that we are
pardoned;
and it is in dying that we are
born to eternal life.

Amen.

PSALM 23

A psalm of David

The LORD is my shepherd;
  there is nothing I lack.
In green pastures you let me
    graze;
  to safe waters you lead me;
  you restore my strength.
You guide me along the right
    path
  for the sake of your name.
Even when I walk through a
    dark valley,

  I fear no harm for you are at
    my side;
  your rod and staff give me courage.

You set a table before me
  as my enemies watch;
You anoint my head with oil;
  my cup overflows.
Only goodness and love will pursue me
  all the days of my life;
I will dwell in the house of the LORD
    for years to come.

PSALM 121

A song of ascents

I raise my eyes toward the
    mountains.
    From where will my help
    come?
My help comes from the
    LORD,
    the maker of heaven and
    earth.

God will not allow your foot
    to slip;
    your guardian does not
    sleep.
Truly, the guardian of Israel
    never slumbers nor sleeps.
The LORD is your guardian;
    the LORD is your shade
    at your right hand.
By day the sun cannot harm
    you,
    nor the moon by night.
The LORD will guard you
    from all evil,
    will always guard your life.
The LORD will guard your coming and going
    both now and forever.

You who dwell in the shelter of the Most High,
   who abide in the shadow of the Almighty,
Say to the LORD, "My refuge and fortress,
   my God in whom I trust."
God will rescue you from the fowler's snare,
   from the destroying plague,
Will shelter you with pinions,
   spread wings that you may take refuge;
   God's faithfulness is a protecting shield.
You shall not fear the terror of the night
   nor the arrow that flies by day,
Nor the pestilence that roams in darkness,
   nor the plague that ravages at noon.
Though a thousand fall at your side,
   ten thousand at your right hand,
   near you it shall not come.
You need simply watch;
   the punishment of the wicked you will see.
You have the LORD for your refuge;
   you have made the Most High your stronghold.
No evil shall befall you,
   no affliction come near your tent.
For God commands the angels
   to guard you in all your ways.

With their hands they shall support you,
   lest you strike your foot against a stone.
You shall tread upon the asp and the viper,
   trample the lion and the dragon.

Whoever clings to me I will deliver;
   whoever knows my name I will set on high.
All who call upon me I will answer;
   I will be with them in distress;
   I will deliver them and give them honor.
With length of days I will satisfy them
   and show them my saving power.

When he saw the crowds, he went up the mountain, and after he had sat down, his disciples came to him.
He began to teach them, saying:

"Blessed are the poor in spirit,
for theirs is the kingdom of heaven.
Blessed are they who mourn,
for they will be comforted.
Blessed are the meek,
for they will inherit the land.
Blessed are they who hunger and thirst for righteousness,
for they will be satisfied.
Blessed are the merciful,
for they will be shown mercy.
Blessed are the clean of heart,
for they will see God.
Blessed are the peacemakers,
for they will be called children of God.
Blessed are they who are persecuted for the sake of
righteousness,
for theirs is the kingdom of heaven.

Blessed are you when they insult you and persecute you and utter every kind of evil against you [falsely] because of me. Rejoice and be glad, for your reward will be great in heaven. Thus they persecuted the prophets who were before you."

—MATTHEW 5:1-1?

1 CORINTHIANS 13

If I speak in human and angelic tongues but do not have love, I am a resounding gong or a clashing cymbal. And if I have the gift of prophecy and comprehend all mysteries and all knowledge; if I have all faith so as to move mountains but do not have love, I am nothing. If I give away everything I own, and if I hand my body over so that I may boast but do not have love, I gain nothing.

Love is patient, love is kind. It is not jealous, [love] is not pompous, it is not inflated, it is not rude, it does not seek its own interests, it is not quick-tempered, it does not brood over injury, it does not rejoice over wrongdoing but rejoices with the truth. It bears all things, believes all things, hopes all things, endures all things.

Love never fails. If there are prophecies, they will be brought to nothing; if tongues, they will cease; if knowledge, it will be brought to nothing. For we know partially and we prophesy partially, but when the perfect comes, the partial will pass away. When I was a child, I used to talk as a child, think as a child, reason as a child; when I became a man, I put aside childish things. At present we see indistinctly, as in a mirror, but then face to face. At present I know partially; then I shall know fully, as I am fully known. So faith, hope, love remain, these three; but the greatest of these is love.

—1 Corinthians 13:1-13